Original title:
Between the Coconut Trees

Copyright © 2025 Creative Arts Management OÜ
All rights reserved.

Author: Vivienne Beaumont
ISBN HARDBACK: 978-1-80581-484-9
ISBN PAPERBACK: 978-1-80581-011-7
ISBN EBOOK: 978-1-80581-484-9

### Dance of the Fragrant Leaves

In the breeze, they sway so free,
Dancing whispers, tickling me.
One leaf trips, another spins,
Nature's laughter, where fun begins.

A cha-cha-cha, oh what a sight,
Leaves twirl round in pure delight.
Branching out, they tease the sun,
Who knew greens could have such fun?

## The Rhythm of Nature's Heart

A flutter here, a rustle there,
Nature plays, without a care.
Vines entwine with joking flair,
Laughter echoes in the air.

A jig of roots, a two-step vine,
Nature's beat is truly divine.
While squirrels groove and branches bend,
This leafy party will never end!

## **Raindrops on Leafy Canopies**

A pitter-patter, a playful game,
Raindrops fall, but never the same.
Dancing round, they swirl and spin,
On each leaf, laughter begins!

Each droplet whispers a little joke,
As puddles form, they're all provoked.
Splashing joy from high above,
Nature's humor, all it loves!

## A Symphony of Shadows

Shadows flicker, a playful tease,
Chasing sunlight in the breeze.
They're in a race, it's quite absurd,
Who knew shadows could be stirred?

A game of tag in the twilight glow,
While gentle winds put on a show.
Laughter rings in this light ballet,
Shadows giggle and sway away!

## Light Play on the Bark

Sunlight dances on the trunk,
Squirrels plotting while they chunk.
Laughing leaves in breezy cheer,
Tickling branches, never fear.

A swing set made of twine and dreams,
Where giggles float like summer streams.
Barking dogs in playful race,
Chasing shadows, a merry chase.

### Nature's Enchanted Murmurs

Whispers of the breezy night,
Lizards prance in pure delight.
Grasshoppers join in a band,
Grooving softly near the sand.

Giggling crickets, oh so sly,
Dancing 'neath a moonlit sky.
A raccoon winks, it gives a shout,
"Check my moves, don't leave me out!"

## The Silence of Verdant Giants

Tall and still, they seem to sigh,
Secrets held as days drift by.
Yet a chipmunk, quick and spry,
Jumps around like it can fly.

Boring branches, they complain,
Until the owls join the train.
A grumpy frog croaks in a groove,
Nature's beat is hard to prove.

## Hidden Treasures in the Twilight

In shadows cast by leafy crowns,
Life's oddities wear funny gowns.
A golden beetle, dressed to impress,
Waddles round like it's a mess.

Bubbles in the twilight glow,
Fireflies spark a gentle show.
Nature winks and blinks with glee,
Silly antics for all to see.

## A Lull in the Tropical Breeze

A monkey swings, a toucan laughs,
A squirrel wears its shiny hats.
On every leaf a giggle's heard,
Nature's comedy, quite absurd.

A parrot squawks its funny tale,
While geckos dance without a scale.
The breeze tickles with playful sways,
In this wild laughter, time delays.

## The Swaying Company of Giants

Palm trees nod in chatter grand,
They gossip with the sun-drenched sand.
"Can you believe that toucan's style?"
The shadows sway and play awhile.

An iguana struts with flair,
"Look at me, do I have a pair?"
Each leaf a stage, each trunk a friend,
In this tall tale, the fun won't end.

## Colors of Shadows at Dusk

As dusk arrives, the colors blend,
Laughter spills without an end.
A firefly taps, "Let's start the show!"
In twilight's glow, our spirits grow.

The shades grow long, the antics begin,
A crab attempts its awkward spin.
With every hue a chuckle bright,
The whispers swirl around the night.

## Singers of the Tropical Night

Beneath the stars, the nightbirds croon,
A chorus sings a silly tune.
A cricket chirps a cheeky line,
In laughter's rhythm, all align.

The night unfolds with jokes and glee,
A frog leaps high, "Come dance with me!"
With every note, the darkness sways,
In this hilarious night ballet.

## Tropical Breezes and Secrets Shared

Sipping drinks while laughter flows,
A parrot mimics, everyone knows.
With hats askew, we dance in pairs,
As crabs join in, without a care.

The sun's a joker, playing tricks,
Waves come crashing, doing flips.
Umbrellas tilt, we chase the shade,
In this paradise, plans are made.

## Rustling Leaves and Whispered Tales

Leaves rustle like gossiping friends,
Tickling toes, this joy never ends.
A monkey swings with cheeky glee,
Stealing snacks like it's a spree.

Shells tell tales of old and new,
Crab races start, a wild crew.
Chasing sandcastles, where did they go?
Their glory fades with a tides' flow.

## Sunset Kisses on Golden Sand

The sun dips low, a brilliant prank,
Splashing colors, oh what a clank!
We scribble hearts in soft, warm heaps,
While nearby, a sandpiper peeps.

The sunset yawns, stretches wide,
Bathing us in warm, golden tide.
A seagull swoops; it steals my fry,
And I just laugh, oh my oh my!

## Nature's Lullaby at Dusk

The night creeps in with subtle cheer,
A chorus sings, can you hear?
Crickets play the violin,
As fireflies dance, a twinkling din.

Tomatoes toss in the evening breeze,
My friend insists they're pirate fees.
With giggles bright, we hold our breath,
For nature's lullabies, dance with zest.

## **Emergence of Dawn in Paradise**

A sleepy sun peeks through the palm,
The roosters cry, the air is calm.
A squirrel in a hat, what a sight,
Dancing on branches, oh what a fright!

A crab in shades walks with flair,
Sneaking right past a curious bear.
Breezy whispers tickle the trees,
Laughter erupts with every breeze.

Coconuts drop like fruity bombs,
The monkeys laugh, oh how it calms.
When dawn emerges, silly and bright,
Every creature wakes, ready for flight!

## Echoed Echoes of Island Solitude

Waves giggle as they kiss the shore,
Jellyfish bounce, but rarely score.
A lone parrot, quite the chat,
Echoes its name, then falls flat!

Seashells gather, a gossip crew,
Whispering tales only they knew.
An octopus juggles, just for fun,
Tentacles twirling—who's won the run?

The island hums a quirky tune,
Bouncing beneath the sleepy moon.
With every echo, a chuckle shared,
In solitude, none are ensnared!

## The Silent Language of Nature

Leaves conversing in rustling tones,
A babbling brook hums soothing drones.
Flowers giggle, in colors they chat,
Even the bumblebees tip their hat!

The wind whispers secrets, soft and sweet,
Dancing with laughter, tapping their feet.
A frog in a top hat leaps with cheer,
His antics make every onlooker near!

In the quiet, there's a jesting grace,
Nature's humor in every place.
From grasses swaying to clouds so quick,
Life's funny riddles come and flick!

## Pacing Steps on Sandy Paths

Footprints dance on the golden sand,
Each step brings giggles, oh so grand.
A kid with a bucket trips in glee,
Splashing the waves, then yelling 'me!'

A sea turtle rolls like it's in a race,
Waddling slowly, but with such grace.
Seagulls squawk in a raucous tune,
Stealing snacks, they'll be gone soon!

Sandy toes and sticky hands,
Building castles with lofty plans.
Laughter mixes with ocean's blast,
On these paths, we forget the past!

## Embraces of Wind and Light

A parrot squawks with glee,
While the wind steals my hat,
I chase it down the shore,
Laughing at my own spat.

Sunbeams dance like kids,
On the trunks and sand,
I slip in my flip-flops,
Oh, this trip is unplanned!

Coconuts wobble high,
As I strike a pose,
One drops and bonks my head,
Laughter, it overflows!

Picnic ants join the fun,
Stealing snacks with flair,
I wave goodbye to them,
While I munch on fresh air.

## Rhythms of the Tropical Day

The sun peeks from behind,
Like a curious cat,
My breakfast's on the ground,
Right where the seagulls sat.

A hammock sways with me,
Like a wobbly boat,
But I'm just a sailor,
With a pirate's wild coat.

The waves sing a soft tune,
While I dance with a breeze,
My flip-flops go flying,
Oh, what a sight to tease!

Drinks spill on my shirt,
A tropical splash game,
I laugh with every sip,
Giggling's my favorite name.

## Timeless Moments in Island Solitude

Birds dive and dart around,
In a feathered ballet,
I sip my fruity drink,
As they steal it away!

Shells sing songs to the sand,
Telling tales of the sea,
I nod as if they speak,
Me, their only marquee.

Sunsets paint the sky,
With canvases so bright,
I trip on my own shadow,
And bid the spear a fright!

Stars peek through the palms,
Winking as they gleam,
Napping on the beach,
Life's but a sandy dream.

## Journeys Through the Green Veil

A lizard eyes my meal,
With a flick of his tail,
I wave like a true friend,
But he's quick on the trail!

Vines twist like silly straws,
Inviting me to climb,
But I fumble and tumble,
And land right on my rhyme!

Monkeys throw smooth coconuts,
In a joking parade,
I dodge a fuzzy bomb,
And into laughter, I'm laid.

Through the jungle I roam,
In this green maze so keen,
Every step's a giggle,
Nature's prankster routine.

## Beneath the Folly of the Green Giants

The green giants sway and twist,
With coconuts that like to miss.
A frisbee launched from branches high,
The kids below just duck and cry.

A monkey steals a snack or two,
While tourists laugh, unsure what to do.
A game of catch with fruit in hand,
Their picnic plans were not quite planned.

A coconut plops, a mighty thud,
Beneath the shade, a splashy flood!
The seagulls snicker, "What a show!"
As people slip in coconut blow!

The green giants grin, and sway in time,
As chaos reigns, oh what a crime!
A funny dance beneath the sun,
In the land where laughter's never done.

## Secrets of the Island Canopy

High above, the leaves conspire,
With whispering winds of mischief dire.
A secret club of squirrels feast,
On nuts and berries, not the least.

They plot and scheme in daylight's glow,
While down below, the tourists flow.
With cameras ready, smiles abound,
But unaware of tricks that surround.

A sudden shower, the birds take flight,
Splashing down with pure delight!
While umbrellas flip like upside-down,
The squirrels cheer, it's time to clown!

In the canopy, the laughter rings,
A little chaos that nature brings.
For secrets shared in leaf and breeze,
Are joys that dance among the trees.

## Dreams in the Tropical Shade

In the shade where dreams take flight,
A hammock sways, almost too tight.
With thoughts of naps and coconut drinks,
While playful lizards watch and wink.

A pineapple rolls, a sneaky game,
As children laugh, and call its name.
"Come back here!" they jump and shout,
As birds above, just sing and flout.

The breeze brings whispers, secrets low,
Of silly antics from below.
A toucan preens with vibrant flair,
While locals giggle, completely unaware.

So dreams are spun in leafy lairs,
Where laughter dances in warm airs.
And every moment feels just right,
In tropical joys that spark delight.

## Serenade of the Tropical Winds

The winds come whistling through the leaves,
With playful tunes that tease and weave.
They tickle noses, tousle hair,
And summon giggles from everywhere.

Banana peels are flying high,
As children chase them, oh my, my!
They slip and slide, a comic trail,
With laughter echoing through the vale.

A parrot squawks, "Look at that man!"
As he attempts the hula plan.
With steady hips, or so he thinks,
The winds just laugh, "Oh, what a twink!"

A serenade of lighthearted charms,
As the island's spirit wraps in its arms.
For in the breeze, pure joy prevails,
With laughter caught on the tropical gales.

## Harmony Under the Glistening Sky

Under the sun, the monkeys play,
Swinging and laughing, brightening the day.
A pineapple hat on a coconut king,
He dances and jigs, makes the seagulls sing.

Palm fronds tickle the breeze so light,
While crab races cause a comical sight.
The tide rolls in with a splish and a splash,
As beach balls bounce in a colorful clash.

Laughter erupts, oh what a bunch,
Of silly sea turtles, sharing their lunch.
Dancing hermit crabs, in their own little strut,
They shake their shells, show us their gut.

As day turns to dusk, the laughter won't cease,
Under the sky, we find our peace.
With giggles and snorts, we sing through the night,
In harmony's rhythm, everything's right.

## Secrets of the Island Grove

In the grove, where secrets brew,
A parrot sings in a silly hue.
With mischievous eyes, he tries to tease,
The wise old tortoise, who just won't squeal.

A game of tag with a wild boar friend,
Around the trees, they twist and bend.
Pineapples roll, in a race for glory,
Each one tells a funny little story.

Coconuts fall with a thud and a clatter,
While cheeky monkeys chatter and scatter.
They boast of their stunts from morning till noon,
A slapstick show, set to a tropical tune.

As night draws near, they gather around,
The secrets shared have no need to be bound.
With chuckles and snorts, they sit side by side,
In the island grove, where fun can't hide.

## **Footprints in the Sand**

Footprints gather, one by one,
Leading to tales of quirky fun.
A crab in a flip-flop takes a stroll,
While beachgoers laugh, feeling quite whole.

Splashing waves, the sound of cheer,
A dolphin jumps high, without any fear.
The shoreline is painted with laughter and play,
As beach buckets dance in the sun's warm ray.

Sandcastles rise like palatial dreams,
Only to fall, but oh how it seems,
That each toppled tower brings a new chance,
For frogs in sombreros to join in the dance.

Under the sky, where wonders expand,
Every footprint tells a tale so grand.
With silly giggles and friends hand in hand,
We write our stories in the soft, warm sand.

## Twilight beneath the Swaying Tops

As twilight falls, colors ignite,
The sky turns purple, a marvelous sight.
Kangaroos dance in a hoppy parade,
While owls crack jokes in the cool evening shade.

The owls wear glasses, quite absurd,
Wise words fall out, you won't be disturbed.
On a tightrope strung from tree to tree,
A squirrel performs, with no fear of free.

Fireflies flicker, a twinkling show,
With laughter and giggles, they steal the glow.
A tip-tap sound as the crickets all play,
Creating a symphony to end the day.

Under the tops, with smiles all abound,
The friendships formed in this magical ground.
With funny stories and hearts full of glee,
We celebrate life, singing wild and free.

## Whispers in the Canopy

In the canopy, monkeys swing,
With laughter as their playful fling.
Coconuts drop like tiny bombs,
While parrots squawk in silly psalms.

A squirrel steals my sandwich quick,
It's a battle of the wits and trick.
The branches giggle in the breeze,
As I hide snacks behind the trees.

Sunshine filters through the leaves,
As cheeky giggles play with eves.
Bamboo sticks bow with a crack,
And I'm left wondering what I lack.

The chatter rises, a silly tune,
Underneath the bright afternoon.
With every rustle, there's a cheer,
In this jungle of joy, I have no fear.

## Shadows on the Shoreline

Shadows dance on sandy trails,
Where crabs wear hats and flip-flop sails.
Surfboards waiting to make a splash,
While the seagulls dive for a trashy stash.

Footprints lead to nowhere nice,
As I trip on shells, more than twice.
Laughing waves tease with a roar,
While pelicans plot from the shore.

The sun tries hard to give a kiss,
But all I get is a sandy miss.
I chase a tide that laughs and rolls,
As sand tickles my happy soles.

Picnics turn to glorious mess,
With ants surrounding my lunch in excess.
Every bite comes with a squeak,
In a comedy sketch, oh so unique.

## **Breeze of the Tropics**

The breeze carries whispers of delight,
As we dance with shadows, taking flight.
A beach ball bounces, oh what a game,
While sunscreen wars leave folks to blame.

Stray dogs prance like they own the place,
Chasing laughter with a joyful face.
I trip and tumble in my flip-flops,
While the breeze giggles, never stops.

Umbrellas tilt at peculiar angles,
As sunburned tourists tell funny jangles.
When coconuts crash with a thud,
We burst into laughter, covered in mud.

Each gust brings a new crazy tale,
With fish that jump like they want a sale.
We sigh and smile as the sun dips low,
Waving to the breeze that steals the show.

## **Silent Dancers of the Palms**

The palms sway softly, a secret sway,
Where silent dancers come out to play.
With each gust, they shake their leaves,
Chatting loudly with swaying thieves.

I try to join in their "silent dance,"
But trip over roots, losing my chance.
Twirling in circles till I'm a mess,
My dance moves cause a leafy distress.

Sun bleeds orange as night creeps near,
While lizards bob to a rhythm unclear.
With every rustle comes a chuckle,
As critters cruise in a whimsical shuffle.

Underneath the Jasmine's sweet breath,
We laugh at moments we won't forget.
In this jungle of giggles, pure delight,
The silent dancers celebrate the night.

## Pockets of Paradise

In the shade, a parrot sings,
While a monkey steals my rings.
Laughter fills the balmy air,
As crabs dance without a care.

Sandy toes and sticky treats,
Dodging gulls that steal my sweets.
Splashing waves, a sunburned nose,
I laugh when coconut water flows.

A hammock swings, a gentle sway,
Snack attacks come out to play.
Tropical hugs from breezy friends,
Here the fun just never ends.

Backyard games and silly pranks,
We toast our drinks and share our thanks.
In this silly, sunlit world,
Joy unfurls like a flag unfurled.

## Honeyed Mornings Beneath the Leaves

Waking up to birds that squawk,
With honey drips atop my clock.
Laughter erupts with every bite,
As ants plan their grand food fight.

Dancing shadows play on sand,
Tropical breezes, oh so grand.
A splash from diving friends nearby,
As water fights reach for the sky.

Sticky fingers and messy hair,
Sun-baked joy beyond compare.
We gather 'round our picnic spread,
To tell tall tales of dreams we've read.

Whimsical moments, sweet and bright,
Under the leaves, we bathe in light.
Days like these are pure delight,
With laughter echoing into night.

## Sunlit Dreams of the Pacific

Under sunbeams, we all play,
Avoiding crabs that snatch our hay.
Children giggle, splashing wide,
As jellyfish take all in stride.

Surfboards tumble, laughter flows,
We flip and flounder like fishy pros.
The ocean's dance is wild and free,
We dive and dash with pure glee.

Seagulls swoop for chips and fries,
While sunscreen makes us look quite wise.
A leap, a splash, a funny fall,
As sunburned faces swell with gall.

In sandy castles, walls of bliss,
We reminisce on each zany kiss.
Oh what fun, this sunny spree,
Forever wild, forever free.

## The Green Symphonies of Evening

As twilight sings a gentle tune,
We laugh and dance beneath the moon.
The critters join, a merry sound,
As fireflies twirl, the night unwound.

Bananas swing upon their vines,
While laughter echoes like fine wines.
With leafy hats, we strut around,
And giggle at the sights we've found.

The stars join in, a cheeky crowd,
Our shenanigans whispered loud.
Storytime with giggly grins,
As night begins and mischief spins.

In the embrace of leafy trees,
We sip our juice and feel the breeze.
Under the green, our hearts take flight,
Creating memories in the night.

## Laughter Echoes in the Palm Trees

In a hammock that swings with a squeak,
A parrot squawks jokes, so unique.
Monkeys throw coconuts down,
As tourists all gather 'round.

A beach ball bounces with flair,
It knocks one man's hat through the air.
Sand flies as the crowd starts to cheer,
The beach is alive with good cheer!

Children chase crabs, what a sight,
One trips and falls, oh what a fright!
Their giggles blend with ocean's roar,
Making memories they'll always adore.

Sunset glimmers, the fun slows down,
With laughter still echoing around.
Under the stars, stories unfold,
In this paradise, joy never gets old.

## **Serenity in the Salty Sprays**

A dog on a surfboard, what a scene,
Chasing a wave, oh so keen!
A fisherman casts with a grin,
But a seagull swoops, out for a win.

Fish tacos served with a wink,
Hot sauce drips as I blink.
A crab considers his escape,
But he just scuttles, oh what a gape!

With each splash, the laughter grows,
As a kid attempts to strike a pose.
Oceans of fun in the briny breeze,
Life tastes sweeter under sunny trees.

As night falls, the tales take flight,
Ghost crabs dance in the moonlight.
Serenity reigns, but what a mess,
With every splash, we are all blessed.

## **Legends in the Shadowed Grove**

There's a tree that holds tales untold,
Of a pirate's treasure and sunsets of gold.
A squirrel darts, with a swish of tail,
As if escaping from some grand tale.

Legend has it a king's lost prize,
Rests beneath branches, hiding from spies.
Kids hunt for it, eyes wide with glee,
Yet it's just old toys, oh what a spree!

Underneath a sunbeam so bright,
Two turtles argue all day and night.
They claim to be the fastest around,
But slow and steady is what we've found.

In this grove, joy's easy to see,
With playful antics, wild and free.
Each rustle brings laughter so brave,
In shady spots, legends misbehave.

## Echoing Laughter in the Boughs

A toucan with a peculiar squawk,
Tells silly jokes as we all dock.
Underneath leafy canopies wide,
We giggle at nature's own fun ride.

A cricket plays nightly serenades,
To dancing shadows in leafy glades.
As we sip juice from quirky cups,
We cheer as one just trips and jumps.

The breeze carries stories far and near,
Of wayward youths, and their silly cheer.
One tries to climb but slips with glee,
Landing softly in a pile of leaves!

When the stars twinkle like a show,
The laughter echoes, soft and low.
In these branches, our hearts take flight,
With every chuckle, life feels so right.

## Twilight Secrets in the Tropics

The monkeys play a game of tag,
As shadows dance and lanterns wag.
A parrot squawks a silly tune,
While crickets hum beneath the moon.

The breeze has secrets, light and sly,
It rustles leaves and whispers by.
A lizard dons a tiny hat,
And tries to charm a passing rat.

The stars join in, a dainty cheer,
As owls hoot jokes, mysteriously clear.
The night is young, let merriment flow,
With laughter echoing in the glow.

So if you see a funny sight,
Just smile and wave beneath the light.
For in this realm of evening's fun,
The laughter echoes, never shun!

## **The Gentle Sway of Nature**

The branches do a wiggly dance,
While critters join in, what a chance!
A squirrel spins like it's a pro,
And slips right into a coconut show.

The wind, it tickles every leaf,
As laughter mingles, oh what relief!
A goat in shades, quite debonair,
Pretends to be a beachside player.

The sun now grins, a cheeky sight,
As shadows play both left and right.
Old trees chuckle, sharing jokes,
While froggies croak, like laughing folks.

With rippling waves that can't be tamed,
Nature's fun, forever famed.
In gentle sways, the world feels bright,
Let's dance along through the night!

## **Rippled Reflections of a Tropical Sunset**

The sun dips low, a flaming ball,
As water shimmers, casting thrall.
A crab in shades takes a long stroll,
While fish below giggle, oh what a goal!

The clouds wear pink, a silly hat,
As seagulls squawk a witty spat.
The sunset winks, a prankster sly,
And dolphins leap, oh my, oh my!

With rippling hues that dance and play,
The evening skies invite the sway.
A turtle waves a flipper high,
Making friends with a kite up in the sky.

Thus twilight breaks, let laughter rise,
In every splash, a joyful surprise.
With nature's joy, we feel the cheer,
Embracing fun, our hearts sincere.

## **Nestled in Nature's Embrace**

A catnap here, a tickle there,
With sleepy eyes and wind-blown hair.
A bunny hops in perfect glee,
While ants march on, a troop at sea.

Old palms sway, a gentle tune,
As squirrels chase beneath the moon.
A raccoon dons its dinner plate,
Inviting all to join the fate.

With flowers blooming, giggles sprout,
While butterflies twirl, roundabout.
A tree frog croaks the silliest call,
In this embrace, we welcome all.

So nestle close, with joy we blend,
In nature's arms, the laughs ascend.
For every laugh, a tale we weave,
In jolly hearts, we all believe!

## Mysteries of the Quiet Shores

On sandy paths where crabs will dance,
The tide rolls in with a goofy glance.
Seashells hiding with secrets untold,
Whispering tales of pirates and gold.

A seagull landed with style and flair,
Stealing sandwiches, without a care.
The surf chuckles, a playful tease,
While I dodge droplets like a sneeze.

Footprints vanish, the wind's a prank,
Slippery stones in shades of dank.
The beach ball's bouncing, we're in a race,
But someone tripped on a flip-flop lace.

The sun sets low, it's time to bake,
Roasting marshmallows, oh what a mistake!
S'mores on faces, giggles galore,
Endless whispers of wanted more.

## **Glimmers of Hope Beneath the Canopy**

Under the leaves where shadows play bright,
Squirrels debate the best nut to bite.
Laughter erupts as branches sway,
A fruit falls down – it's lunch today!

Raccoons arrive, with mischief in mind,
Tenacious thieves, the sneaky kind.
Berries in hand, we start a feast,
Their tiny paws sell dreams, at least.

The sun peeks through with a cheeky grin,
While frogs audition for a ribbiting win.
We waltz through bushes that tickle our toes,
Each giggle echoing where the wild winds blow.

As evening falls, the fireflies blink,
Our shadows dance, and we share a wink.
The night's our canvas, let's paint it bright,
With tales and snacks that fill delight.

## Celestial Passages Over Island Dreams

Stars twinkle like nuts in a bowl,
Each one winks, 'Hey, come ride my shoal!'
A boat drifts by, with a comet's tail,
As fish play cards, how's that for a tale?

Mermaids gossip with dolphins in tow,
About humans and their silly shows.
The moon chimes in, a cheeky old chap,
'Dance on the waves, avoid the flap!'

Clouds roll in, a circus arrives,
With juggling raindrops and laughing skies.
We shout "hooray" with each splash we make,
Catching the giggles in a big, wide lake.

The night winds down, it's time for a rest,
But dreams will carry on with their quest.
So let's sail onward, the world's awake,
For laughter's the treasure we'll always stake.

## Intimate Whispers of Leafy Sanctuaries

In lush green hideouts where laughter grows,
Butterflies dance, but nobody knows.
The fruit's a chatterbox, ripe for a bite,
With shimmer and giggles, it's pure delight.

A monkey swings down, wearing a hat,
Challenging us to a silly spat.
His charms are unmatched, with antics galore,
As we cheer him on, we're begging for more.

The shadows mingle, secrets they keep,
While we sip on coconuts, unafraid of sleep.
Laughter erupts like popcorn in air,
Even trees seem to chuckle, it's quite a fair!

As night settles in, lanterns ignite,
We'll swap our stories until it's light.
With heartbeats and whispers, we cherish the night,
In leafy enclaves, where dreams take flight.

## **The Canopy's Calm Embrace**

High above the sandy shores,
Monkeys swing and dance in scores.
They wear shades, with style so bold,
As they share jokes that never get old.

Squirrels race with nuts in tow,
Playing tag while palm leaves blow.
Their laughter mixes with the breeze,
Creating joy with such great ease.

A parrot squawks a cheeky rhyme,
Right on cue, just in time.
The sun peeks through with a goofy grin,
As the funny games begin to spin.

In this canopy, life's a show,
With every swing, the silly flows.
While below, the world spins fast,
Above, the joy forever lasts.

## Kaleidoscope of Life Above

Up in the trees, a colorful sight,
Birds in feathered costumes take flight.
They breakdance on a vibrant leaf,
Giggling loud, beyond belief!

Bouncing beetles, tiny acrobats,
Juggling berries, while wearing hats.
They tumble down, land on a vine,
Cheering on their friend, divine.

A lizard flexes, shows off his flair,
Strutting the branch with debonair air.
Suddenly he slips, the crowd gasps wide,
But he just laughs, takes it in stride.

Nature's circus, a vibrant tease,
Frolicking critters, oh, such a breeze!
In this tapestry of fun and light,
Life's a party, oh what a sight!

## Whispers of the Tropics

The breeze whispers tales of things unseen,
Where silly shadows twist and preen.
Treetops giggle, branches sway,
As monkeys plot their next grand play.

A sloth, ever slow, rolls his eyes,
While toucans debate the best surprise.
They snag pineapples tossed with flair,
Dancing to rhythms no one can bear.

Palm leaves rustle, sharing some shade,
As a chubby raccoon tries to invade.
He stumbles, trips on his way to fame,
Leaving behind his snack, what a shame!

Under this sky, with laughter around,
The most curious tales are easily found.
In playful harmony, life intertwines,
As the tropics share their endless designs.

## **Dance of the Palm Fronds**

The palm fronds sway to a rhythm divine,
Hosting a party, oh how they shine!
Crickets chirp, keeping the beat,
While fireflies twirl on tiny feet.

A crab on the sand does a quick shuffle,
And joins in the jig with a happy scuffle.
His friends cheer as they stomp and clap,
Uniting under the moon's big lap.

With every gust, the laughter grows,
As waves crash, and merriment flows.
In this palm dance, no room for sorrows,
Just funny antics and sunny tomorrows!

When the night falls, the fun won't cease,
For nature's circus lives in peace.
And as dawn peeks, all blink with glee,
For tomorrow's dance beneath the tree.

## **Oasis of Serenity**

In a leafy haven, birds take flight,
Chasing shadows, what a sight!
A monkey swings with great delight,
While sipping coconuts, oh what a plight!

Fronds waving like an old man's hair,
Swaying gently, without a care,
The sun peeks in, a golden glare,
A lizard sneezes, folks stop and stare!

Palm trees giggle, what a muse,
As tourists dance in worn-out shoes,
Sand gets stuck, it's like a ruse,
But laughter echoes, it's the best excuse!

Under this canopy of fun,
Life's a vacation, never done,
Forget your worries, come and run,
In this paradise, everyone can shun!

## Echoes of the Tropical Breeze

Where the breeze plays a funny tune,
A crab dances beneath the moon,
He struts and stumbles with a swoon,
All in time with the ocean's croon!

Seagulls squawk like they've gone mad,
As children chase, never a tad,
Falling down, they giggle, glad—
Sandcastles crumble, but they're not sad!

Coconuts juggle, oh what a sight,
One lands on a head, oh what a fright!
Laughing out loud, it feels so right,
In this dream where day meets night.

Frogs jump in rhythm with waves that sing,
Breezes blow love, oh what a fling!
Amidst the laughter, joy takes wing,
In this land where the silly reigns king!

## **Nature's Breath in the Shade**

Under canopies where giggles bloom,
Chasing critters, they're bound to zoom!
A squirrel steals a snack, oh the gloom,
While children yell, 'Do you smell that perfume?'

The breeze teases, pulling hats away,
Oh look, another fashion faux pas today!
Flip-flops flop, a dog starts to play,
In this crazy mess, who needs to stay?

Crickets chirp in a silly song,
While the sun keeps flirting all day long,
Nature's riddle, oh where do we belong?
Between giggles, life feels like a throng!

So let's gather 'neath the joyous trees,
With lemonade and whispers of peace,
Sprinkled fun as time seems to freeze,
In this shade, laughter is the main tease!

## Guardians of the Island

The palms stand guard, like old, wise friends,
Holding secrets that never ends,
Tickling the sky as the fun transcends,
While the island dances, laughter bends!

A toucan's beak, oh what a show,
He mimics folks, putting on a glow,
A party of antics, just so you know,
Banana peels slipping, neat on the low!

Fishermen's tales, tall as the tide,
With fish that grow wings, what a ride!
Laughter echoes, they can't hide,
Sharing stories, with every stride!

So join the fun, let worries flee,
In this haven, wild and free,
The island chuckles, come and see,
With guardians of joy, life's jubilee!

## A Tapestry Woven of Leaves

In the shade, a parrot yells,
A squirrel steals my snacks, oh well!
Laughter echoes, light and free,
Nature's laugh is good company.

With a coconut, I take my aim,
Miss the tree, but hit a dame.
She laughs and throws a fruit my way,
'Next time, try the mango play!'

Lizard dances on a thin vine,
Making all the ladies pine.
He slips and lands upon my head,
Now I've got a friend instead!

The sun dips down, a golden tease,
We all gather 'neath the breeze.
With jokes and jests, spirits soar,
Every moment brings out more!

## **Tropical Harmony at Daybreak**

The rooster crows, a clumsy tune,
He thinks he's quite the morning boon.
Waves laugh softly on the sand,
As we all stretch out, unplanned.

A monkey swings with reckless glee,
He steals my hat, oh, quite a spree!
I chase him down, it's quite the race,
He grins, then wipes my smile off my face.

Bright sunbeams wink from leafy throne,
While crabs scuttle on their own.
We share our tales, from near and far,
With coconuts as our bizarre stars.

Every morning, laughter wakes,
With ocean songs and silly quakes.
Together we make quite the crew,
Adventures in shades of green and blue!

## Cascades of Green and Blue

A splash of water, oh, what a scene,
The fish called out, 'You're looking mean!'
Turtles giggle as they glide,
While I fumble, looking for pride.

With a flip-flop lost, I stomp about,
The island's laughter starts to sprout.
Break a shell, and what do you see?
A crab emerges, as proud as can be.

The breeze teases, it calls my name,
But the sun's heat is not a game.
I dive right in, a splashy show,
While my best friend yells, 'Take it slow!'

In the water, we spin like fools,
Ocean waves, our endless pools.
With laughter loud, we bid the day,
In this place where fun holds sway!

## **Enchantment in the Island Air**

Breezes whisper through the trees,
They share secrets with the bees.
A mushroom laughs under my feet,
And makes me stumble, oh, what a feat!

A parade of ants struts proud,
They march to tunes, oh, quite loud!
With snacks they steal, I share a laugh,
While a butterfly cheers on their path.

Dreams of coconuts drift on by,
An iguana stretches, oh my, oh my!
He poses like a superstar,
While we cheer him from near and far.

As day turns dusk with vibrant flair,
We toast to joy found in the air.
Together, with smiles wide and bright,
We revel till the end of light!

## **A Tangle of Green and Gold**

A monkey swings with all his might,
Chasing coconuts that dance in flight.
He'll juggle them while standing tall,
Oops! There goes another — down they fall.

The parrots squawk their raucous tune,
While crabs play tag beneath the moon.
The leaves are rustling with their cheer,
Who knew this place could bring such fear!

Giggling children run amok,
In search of treasure, let's unlock.
With slippery feet and muddy prints,
They dash around, their laughter hints.

A picnic blend of fruit and fun,
Sunburnt cheeks, but still they run.
In a tangle of green and gold,
Adventures spark with tales retold.

## Oasis of Calm in the Tropics

An iguana plays the cool big shot,
Sunning in a patch that's way too hot.
A breeze complains and waves hello,
As pineapples roll down just for show.

The hammock sways like a lazy cat,
As cousin Fred sits, tipped like that.
A drink spills over, splashing bright,
He's swimming in his own delight!

Rats hold meetings with the stars,
Whispering secrets of the far bazars.
While flip-flops flop on sandy ground,
The laughter echoes all around.

In this oasis, let's recline,
With fruity drinks that truly shine.
We'll savor snacks and let joy bloom,
As butterflies chase away the gloom.

## Melodies of the Coastal Breeze

With a ukulele, a crab strums away,
Hoping to start a beachside soirée.
Turtles tap their feet to the beat,
As seagulls declare, "This song is neat!"

The wind carries whispers, giggles abide,
While fish in the bay put on a slide.
Wave after wave, they curl and play,
Dancing along until they sway.

A sandcastle contest builds up a fuss,
Judges are ants — they won't make a fuss.
The whimsy of laughter spreads so wide,
Under the sun, we take enormous pride.

In melodies sweet, a joyful parade,
Every note a moment that won't jade.
As we twirl and spin, let spirits soar,
On this beach of laughter, who could want more?

## The Dance of Shadows and Light

In the twilight glow, shadows sneak,
While geckos plot their silly streak.
A dance-off starts on the sandy floor,
As fireflies blink and spirits roar.

Bamboo flicks play a rhythmic song,
As the breeze joins in, it won't be long.
Sneaky crickets hop with grace,
In a playful chase, they set the pace.

Marshmallows roast on a little flame,
But someone's face is covered in shame.
A s'more mishap with chocolate galore,
Now sticky fingers we can't ignore!

As the stars twinkle with cheeky glee,
The night is alive, can't you see?
In shadows and light, laughter ignites,
This dance of joy fills endless nights.

**Stillness Under the Swaying Giants**

A breeze dances with a leaf,
Nearby, a squirrel steals some chief.
He's plotting mischief on the ground,
While shadows waltz, all round and round.

A bird up high sings tunes so sweet,
While ants parade in steady beat.
Can't understand their little fuss,
While I enjoy my coconut plus.

The sun peeks down, a lazy stare,
As I recline without a care.
Why run around when you can chill?
The world can wait; I'll sip my swill.

Laughter echoes through the trees,
As crabs hold court, discussing fees.
Their tiny claws and grandiose tales,
In this quiet nook, all prevails.

## Dappled Sunlight and Ocean's Song

With waves that giggle on the shore,
I find a flip-flop, what a chore!
The sea foam tickles at my toes,
As wind playing pranks, mischievous grows.

Sea gulls drop in for a snack,
Stealing crumbs right from my pack.
I chase them off with laughter loud,
While clouds form shapes that make me proud.

The horizon sings, a playful tune,
While sunbeams dance like a cartoon.
With each sip of my fruity drink,
I ponder life—then stop and wink.

Oh, the antics of the day,
With sandy feet, I'm here to stay!
A little splash, a giggling fit,
In this paradise, I fully commit.

## Painted Skies Over Island Shores

Sunset splashes colors so bold,
With hues of pink, like stories told.
The horizon winks, a cheeky grin,
As I ponder how to dive in.

A hammock sways, my favorite spot,
Not a care, just bliss I've got.
A drink in hand, the waves do play,
While I daydream the hours away.

Laughter bursts among the sand,
As kids and puppies run hand in hand.
One slips, another falls with grace,
In this comedy, we find our place.

The stars peek out, a twinkling joke,
And laughter rings from every folk.
Tonight we feast on tropical fruits,
In this paradise, life always suits.

## Driftwood Whispers and Salty Air

Driftwood tells tales of ocean's past,
Of sailors bold and shadows cast.
I sit, intrigued, in this cozy nook,
And sip sweet tea from a funny book.

The scent of salt, a gentle tease,
As breezes come, they laugh with ease.
A napkin flutters, what a sight,
It joins the dance; it's quite the flight.

Flip-flops chill; the tide rolls in,
As seashells gather, sometimes kin.
A conch shell's blare, a sassy sound,
Echoes of laughter all around.

With every wave, a tickling jest,
This shore provides the very best.
In salty air, we sway and cheer,
Under the skies, we lose our fear.

## Sunlight's Embrace in the Green

Under bright rays, the shadows dance,
Lizards sunbathe—what a chance!
Silly monkeys swing with glee,
While I sip nectar, just let it be.

Grasshoppers join the wild parade,
Bouncing about, they seem unafraid.
Rains loom, yet here we stay,
Juggling fruit in a carefree way.

Clouds drift slowly, what a sight,
They look like giants in a pillow fight.
Yet here in laughter, we find our bliss—
A moment captured, we wouldn't miss!

With coconut hats perched on our heads,
We dance around, dodging all the threads.
The sun's warm hug is hard to evade,
But who cares? Let's keep this charade!

## Lullabies from the Fronds

Whispering leaves, they sing so sweet,
A lullaby for our dancing feet.
The crabs tap out a funny beat,
As the sunset paints our retreat.

Tangled in roots, we find a place,
To giggle softly, without a trace.
A squirrel joins with a cheeky grin,
Stealing snacks—we'll let him win!

Breezes pass, a playful tease,
Making palmiers dance with ease.
Tickling the branches, soft and light,
Turning the mundane into delight.

A chorus of joy amidst the green,
Funny faces unseen, yet keen.
With every hum and fluttered sigh,
We weave tales where laughter can fly!

## Murmurs Among the Trunks

Gnarled old trunks wear laughter's grace,
With whispers of nuts in a frantic race.
Frogs croak jokes, their timing just right,
Echoing giggles as day turns to night.

Swaying vines join in the jest,
Telling the world we're simply blessed.
A troupe of ants, they march and tease,
Crafting a conga line with ease!

With every rustle, a tale unfolds,
Of forgotten dreams and woodland gold.
Silly shadows skip on the floor,
Joining the fun—who could ask for more?

In this green realm, we frolic and play,
Making memories that never fray.
Laughter's magic weaves through the bark,
Lighting our hearts, igniting the spark!

## Dreams in the Leafy Arch

Under the leaves, we share our dreams,
Like silly fish caught in bright streams.
Footloose and fancy, we take our flight,
Swinging through branches till it's night.

Banana peels act as slides,
We laugh hard at our comical rides.
A parrot caws, with tales to tell,
Of a coconut prince—oh, do ring a bell!

We carve out laughter in every nook,
With goofy poses, we play our book.
The nighttime hum, a comforting tune,
Under starlit skies, we swoon and swoon.

So here we remain, in joy we bask,
With dreams and smiles—no need to ask.
In leafy arches, we find our rest,
With funny stories, we are truly blessed!

## Harmony of the Island Whispers

The crabs held meetings with the ants,
Discussing who wears the best pants.
A troupe of geckos played the lead role,
In a drama about a lost goldfish's soul.

The breeze told jokes to the swaying fronds,
While the parrots chimed in with odd blondes.
They laughed at the sun who tripped on a cloud,
And turned a bit pink, it was quite loud!

A lizard slid by with a charming grin,
Claiming he'd won the great dance-off win.
But the toucans just rolled their bright eyes,
Saying, "We all know you hide from the pies!"

Under a shower of feathers and light,
The island folks danced on into the night.
With a coconut drumbeat, the party would flow,
As the moon tried to steal the whole funny show.

## Voices of the Swaying Silk

A turtle complained about a slow bus,
While a crab snapped back, "You're the one who's a fuss!"
The palm leaves giggled at the whole silly fight,
In this paradise realm where all was just right.

An octopus painted in hues far and wide,
Thought he'd start a fashion run, oh what a ride!
But the fishes just swam off to catch a good nap,
Leaving the crab with a deli style cap.

Two monkeys swung by on a vine held so tight,
One missed the branch and cried, "What a fright!"
But laughter erupted with each slip and fall,
As the island embraced the joy of it all.

At dusk, island tunes drifted high into space,
With giggles and grins, every soul found their place.
Coconuts chuckled, feeling grateful and free,
In this land of mischief, joy, and glee.

## Explorations Beneath the Tropical Canopy

While exploring the jungle with map upside down,
A monkey grinned wide, wearing a crown.
"Follow me, humans, I know the best tree!"
But they found only coconuts thrown at their knee.

The snakes decided to open a school,
Teaching the lizards about swimming in pools.
But each class ended with a slippery slide,
Leaving all reptiles cheeks chubby with pride.

A kid took a dive to chase after a fish,
Unaware he had just made a big, squishy mish!
The fish bubbled up, "You'll need better shoes!"
As the turtles shouted, "Just have a good snooze!"

With laughter echoing through trees tall and green,
The jungle became a circus, lively and keen.
When the sun came to peek through the leaves up above,
All critters rejoiced, sharing laughter and love!

## Fluttering Secrets of the Palm Grove

Whispers of gossip through the leaves did sweep,
About a bird who couldn't find sleep.
Humming a tune, he thought he'd impress,
But ended up tangled in his own feathered mess.

The slow sloth hosted a party too late,
Inviting some friends, but they missed the date.
"Come tomorrow," he sighed, with a shrug and a yawn,
"Or just come for lunch, when the night is gone!"

Squirrels were spinning in dance with delight,
While beetles complained, "We're tired, we might!
Right after a nap, we'll join you again,
But keep it down low, we're not a big fan!"

So laughter bubbled within the palm's embrace,
As critters spun stories in this merry place.
With jokes going round and the limited snores,
The island thrived in funny folklore.

## Shadows on Sandy Shores

A crab scuttles past in a hurry,
Wearing a shell that's far too flurry.
He waves hello with a quirky glance,
Dancing to waves like he knows how to prance.

Seagulls squawk with a feathery flair,
Stealing fries from a beachgoer's chair.
Sunbathers laugh at the cheeky brigade,
Chasing their shadows, the fun never fades.

Flip-flops fly in an accidental arc,
Someone yells, 'That's my snack, you shark!'
A dog runs off with the last hot dog,
Leaving a picnic in a silly fog.

With laughter and squeals, the beach's alive,
Creating joy as we all dive and thrive.
In shadows of fun, summer seems to last,
As waves crash gently, our worries are past.

## Beneath the Canopy's Embrace

Chill with coconuts, a luscious treat,
But I got one that got up on its feet!
Rolling away with a mischievous grin,
I chase after it, oh where to begin?

Mangoes gossip from a high-up branch,
'We're the stars of this tropical dance!'
While squirrels debate on the nutty rate,
Making life hard for the poor nut crate.

A toucan, joyful, with colors so bright,
Challenges me to a fruit-flinging fight.
My aim is quite poor; I hit a nearby tree,
While the toucan cackles, saying, 'Look at me!'

So we gather 'round for laughter and cheer,
Underneath the leaves, the fun's so near.
With every fruit drop and silly mistake,
Beneath the lush greens, we giggle and shake.

## Lullabies of Swaying Palms

A palm tree winks with a leafy embrace,
'Nap time!' it calls, with a slow, swaying grace.
But who can sleep with the monkeys' loud play?
Singing their tunes in a cheeky array.

Crickets join in with their nightly tune,
While starfish watch from the sandy dune.
A night owl hoots as if in delight,
Chasing after dreams in the pale moonlight.

The breeze tells tales of the day's silly fun,
As creatures and giggles all come as one.
Under the canopy, dreams take their flight,
With lullabies swaying 'til the morning light.

Who needs sheep when you've got this crew?
Napping with pals, everything feels new.
In the hush of the night, laughter will bloom,
While swaying palm leaves guard the room.

## Echoes of the Ocean Breeze

The ocean whispers secrets to the shore,
'Bring your sunscreen; I've got so much more!'
Tanned turtles giggle, making quite the scene,
Rolling in waves like a summertime dream.

A fish pops up, wearing sunglasses with flair,
'Join the fish party! We sing without care.'
A dolphin leaps in with a flip and a splash,
Turning our beach day to an ocean bash!

Crabs join the dance with their sideways groove,
As strange beach games make everyone move.
With each wave crashing, the laughter won't cease,
In echoes of fun, we find our peace.

As night sets in, and stars start to peek,
We'll tell silly tales till the next day's peak.
For what's a beach day without some good cheer?
In the place where the ocean feels oh-so-near.

www.ingramcontent.com/pod-product-compliance
Lightning Source LLC
Chambersburg PA
CBHW072128070526
44585CB00016B/1580